WHAT IF...?

Freedom from Self-Limiting Beliefs

MARIE SCOTT

Published by Goldcrest Books International Ltd
www.goldcrestbooks.com
publish@goldcrestbooks.com

ISBN: 978-1-911505-40-2 (paperback)

ISBN: 978-1-911505-41-9 (ebook)

For the love of David, Dylan, and Harley

TABLE OF CONTENTS

"The important thing is not to stop questioning. Curiosity has its own reason for existence"

Albert Einstein

INTRODUCTION

The Power Of The Question Mark

"In Zen mind, all solutions arise within the question"

The inspiration for the *What if...?* format of this book comes from noticing the transformative power of asking questions. Questioning things as they are gives us the opportunity to create something new. Something better. We are all creating in every moment, whether consciously or unconsciously, through our beliefs. Even if the majority of what we are creating is unwanted. However, by acknowledging our beliefs and opening up to new possibilities, we can let go of those that are no longer working for us and begin to choose ones that do. Ones that enhance our lives, and the lives of others. And, as we liberate ourselves from the prison of our own beliefs, we inspire others to free themselves. The introduction of a question mark where there was previously only a fixed perception allows a state of Openness, Flexibility, Unfolding, Ease, Grace, Flow, Infinite Possibility and Limitless Potential to arise. Now we get to consciously create our experience.

"A belief is just a thought you keep thinking."

Esther Hicks

We often mistake beliefs for truth. Seeing them as dependable and enduring. Absolute. Yet, with so many contrasting belief systems across the planet, how can we discern which are true? It's easy to assume that whatever *we* believe is true...otherwise, why would we bother believing it? For the most part, the answer may be because we've been taught or told to believe it by someone else. From the moment we are born (and perhaps beyond), our beliefs are continually being formed and shaped by our familial, educational, cultural, and religious experiences, as well as many other factors. Left unquestioned, unexplored, we may continue to hold these beliefs for life. On closer examination, however, it becomes apparent that beliefs vary in many ways. Not only culturally, but over time. What was held as truth a thousand years ago, in the last century, a decade ago, or even yesterday can change as our awareness expands. As we become more enlightened. Ultimately, we might well wonder *Why bother having any beliefs at all?*

Our beliefs can work for or against us. On the one hand, they can make us fearful. Keep us small. Limit us. Drive us apart from and set us against each other. Make us self-righteous. They can be used to justify judging, controlling and even killing one another. On the other hand, in this seemingly unpredictable world, they can bring a welcome sense of order and structure to our lives. A feeling of ground beneath our feet. Security, meaning and purpose. Shared beliefs can create a sense of connection and belonging. Over the centuries, it has been expressed by numerous people in various ways that *whether we believe something is possible or not, we are right*. What is perhaps most powerful about such a statement is the implication we have a choice. Opening us to the possibility that we can choose our beliefs, and that, through our beliefs, we create our reality.

Our beliefs are said to be held within the cells of our body. In the case of self-limiting beliefs, then, one might describe them not only as biological cells, but prison cells! Holding us captive. Fortunately, not only are we the imprisoned, we are also the prison guard. Holding the key to our own release.

Some self-limiting beliefs can be released straight away. A *lightbulb moment*, as it were. Other, more ingrained, beliefs may require us to repeatedly cultivate awareness. Many of our beliefs have developed over the course of a lifetime. It is no surprise, then, that they can sometimes take a little time to be fully released. There is no rush. In fact, it can be most transformative to give ourselves the time and space we need to transition...even into greater freedom! Trying to release ourselves quickly can be jarring. It is, essentially, a lifetime process. We may as well enjoy the ride! Having said this, I have found the 'quickest' path to liberation is extreme gentleness. Treating oneself with compassion and loving kindness, even when (especially when) we notice we are being self-critical. Not judging oneself for being judgemental, criticising oneself for being critical, nor berating oneself for berating oneself but stopping the cycle of self-abuse, right here in the moment. By loving oneself, whatever.

You do not have to agree with any of the What if...? questions in this book.

The questions in this book are ones that came up for me in response to my own limiting thoughts which I then flipped on their head and turned into their *What if...?* opposite. One-a-day for ninety days. The questions vary in intensity from soothing, to amusing, to stimulating, to downright crazy-seeming. You do not have to agree with any of the *What if...?* questions in this book. That's not the point. They are simply here to help you explore and develop awareness of your current thoughts and beliefs. An opportunity to open up to greater possibilities. You may notice recurring themes, contradictions and paradoxes. All good fodder for expanding consciousness!

Feel free to use this book in any way that suits you.

Although there is a certain flow to the order, each question also stands perfectly alone. So, whether you prefer to experience the journey from beginning to end, or whether you simply want to dip in, as and when and where you please, the choice is yours. The ninety questions can also be used as 'oracle cards' for instant reflection. Simply bring awareness to what is troubling you in the present moment, randomly choose a number between 1 and 90, or close your eyes and flick through the pages until you feel the urge to stop, and read that question. Noticing whether anything shifts or lightens up — bodily, mentally, emotionally or indeed, spiritually. I often use this method myself, and never cease to be amazed by how often just the right question seems to show up.

The page-a-day aspect of the book emerged as a result of reading Robert Christopher's *Zen and the Pen* (Cottage Press 2013), in which the reader is guided to write their own book. Journalling a page of whatever it is one feels passionate about for ninety days. He speaks of the potency of working with the natural rhythms of nature, such as writing between the equinox and solstice. Christopher also encourages cultivating *Zen Mind*, and writing from this space. As I experienced Zen Mind for myself, this is what appeared on the page:

> *I notice, in Zen Mind, it seems, all solutions exist. Easily and effortlessly. Almost as questions arise, so do the answers. In Zen Mind, solutions arise within the question.*

And so this book came into being! If you, too, decide to journal your thoughts, remember, whether it's a page-a-day, a page-a-week, writing at certain times of the day, at inspiring locations, or even flowing with the phases of the moon, finding a way of writing that suits you can be a joy in itself.

> *A big clue to self-limiting blocks are those responses that begin with "Yeah, but...!"*

So, *what if*...we really can liberate ourselves simply with awareness? Imagine the possibility. How does it sound? Miraculous, ridiculous, awesome, crazy, exciting, outrageous, scary? All of the above? It's most beneficial to be truthful with ourselves here. If it seems like a ridiculous notion, that's fine. In fact, it's great. The whole point of this book is to actively explore ideas that *challenge* our current beliefs. This is how we grow, expand, evolve. Journalling whatever is coming up is a great way to get a handle on any worries, concerns, limitations and blocks as they arise. Creating space to be completely honest with oneself. A big clue to self-limiting blocks are those responses that begin with *"Yeah, but....!"* These sentences tend to indicate a level of resistance within us. Yet, whatever it is we are resisting is often the very thing that empowers us. The key to our self-liberation.

Unconsciously venting concerns from a place of fear often creates painful consequences for both ourselves and others. Ultimately, keeping us trapped in a cycle of misery. Consciously voicing fears and blocks, on the other hand, can be deeply transformative. Helping us identify and release self-limiting beliefs rather than simply recycling them.

As strange as it may sound, liberating ourselves can be a little daunting at first. And with sayings like *Curiosity killed the cat!*, who can blame us for feeling a little apprehensive around exploring change? It is what many of us crave and yet when we experience our first taste, it can feel a little overwhelming. Like we're a balloon about to be untethered. Exciting and scary at the same time. It is great that our emotions, and particularly our fears, are coming up to the surface to be released, but at times like this, it is good to take a step back and ground ourselves. Put the book down. Do something else. There are infinite ways to do this, but some of the most helpful are, thankfully, also the simplest.

Notice the breath.

Drink water.

Be in nature.

Journal.

Do anything else that works for you.

Beyond this book, you may wish to further explore your own limiting thoughts and beliefs by challenging their validity and creating your own *What if...?* alternatives. There is a simple guide to help with this at the back of the book.

What if...?

1

What if...whatever is happening right now is perfect?

Whenever our lives appear to be far from perfect, asking ourselves this question can be particularly potent. It can relax and open us up to the possibility that we may not need to control every aspect of our lives as we're often led to believe. *Phew!* Reminding us that, whatever we're experiencing, there may be a bigger picture.

What if...whatever is happening right now is perfect? What if all we desire to experience is already flowing towards us effortlessly, but we simply get in our own way? Perhaps even blocking the flow with our plans and our expectations of how things ought to be? What difference would it make to our life, knowing that whatever is happening for us right now...is perfect?

2

*What if...*it's OK to feel 'flat' sometimes?

These days, especially when it comes to wellbeing, there is a lot of emphasis on positive thinking. Generally speaking, it is a helpful approach to life. However, as with any approach or practice, we can use it to our benefit or to our detriment. Sometimes we use the very tool intended to bring joy into our lives to beat ourselves over the head with instead. *Why can't I be more positive? What am I doing wrong? What's the matter with me?*

*What if...*it's OK to feel 'flat' sometimes? What if true positivity includes accepting, allowing and appreciating our flatness too? Realising it's here as a message. A friend, even. A sense of flatness can be a sign we have been overworking and overthinking. A sign it's time to rest. Take a breather. Let out all the *hot air*. In other words, allow ourselves to *deflate* for a while.

3

*What if...*slowing down creates more time?

Have you ever had the feeling there simply aren't enough hours in the day? When there is so much pressure that your body tenses up, your breath shortens, and your mind races in preparation for that day's to-do list? *Go!* Once the panicky feeling of overwhelm has set in, the last, and I mean the last thing we feel able to do is slow down or stop. *Are you crazy? Do you know how much I have to do today? I can't afford to slow down!*

*What if...*slowing down creates more time? Perhaps by stopping and taking a breath, we allow the tension of our fight-or-flight responses to settle, which in turn allows the fog of overwhelm to clear. By affording ourselves a moment of serenity, we might see how to accomplish our tasks with greater ease and grace. Able to make wiser, more efficient and therefore pleasurable choices. What if, by taking our time we actually create time?

4

What if...pressuring ourselves doesn't really help?

Sure, pressuring ourselves often gets things done, but does it make us happy? Yes, to the extent that we feel good about having completed a task, but have we enjoyed the journey to completion? Never mind what the stress might be doing to our health!

*What if...*pressuring ourselves doesn't really help? What if we don't have to apply pressure to get things done? What if loving ourselves is more efficient? When we're in a relaxed and loving state, we tend to see more clearly. Solutions come with ease. And we get to enjoy ourselves along the way!

5

What if...letting something collapse allows something better to take its place?

The tension and pressure of trying to hold it all together can be unbearable at times. Like trying to keep a dozen juggling balls in the air...whilst walking a tightrope! Whether it be a situation, a relationship or an old belief, the thought of letting go of even one of them can bring up immense fear and dread. As if dropping one ball might make the whole lot collapse.

What if...letting something collapse allows something better to take its place? What if collapse is the best thing that could happen right now? In our best interests. What if something better can only come in after the old has been released? Once space has been cleared. It can take infinite courage to let go. A real *leap of faith*. But who knows what wonders are waiting for us on the other side?

6

What if...we can access whatever we want in the here and now?

When we want something in life it can often feel out of reach. Over there. Someday. The wait can be agonising. Sometimes the more we want it, the more distant it can feel. But what if what we are ultimately chasing is a feeling? What if that car is simply a yearning for freedom? A partner; a desire for love. A business; a longing for more purpose. A house; a wish for security.

What if...we can access whatever we want in the here and now? What if by surrendering in the moment, choosing to physically relax body and mind, we can access the experience we want? Tap into our inherent freedom. Feel love in our heart. Realise a sense of purpose. Notice a feeling of security arising from within. What if we discover this is more than enough? And yet, what if in this space of consistent relaxation, the car, the partner, the business, the house show up anyway?

7

*What if...*all the answers we need are within?

When faced with a problem, we are generally accustomed to following the advice of experts. Whether it's a financial, health, relational, business, or spiritual concern, we often imagine they know best. Listening to expert advice can be helpful. Sometimes, however, it can create more confusion! Especially when the 'experts' can't agree with one another, or the information keeps changing. How many times have we heard that a particular food is good for us, only to hear the following week that it is not? And vice versa.

*What if...*all the answers we need are within? *But I'm no expert!* we might say. Perhaps not in that particular field but what if, ultimately, we are the experts on *us?* Not about every one else, but regarding *our* life. This doesn't stop us listening to what other people have to say, but it might involve paying attention to that whisper within. That constant source of inner wisdom. As long as we are quiet and still enough to hear it.

8

*What if...*our vulnerability is a gift?

Vulnerability is not usually first on our list of 'qualities to develop'. In fact, it is not often considered a quality at all. Rather, a weakness. Something to be avoided at all costs. From a young age, we are told to *be strong* and *put on a brave face*. But what if putting on a brave face is keeping us separate from the very assistance we need right now? What if we are doing such a good job at being strong that no one notices when we are struggling? No one realises the depth of suffering within. Could we blame them?

*What if...*our vulnerability is a gift? Having the courage to admit our sense of vulnerability to ourselves puts us in touch with our humanness. Being in touch with our humanness puts us in touch with everybody else's. Our sense of humanity is what connects us on this planet. It's how compassion for ourselves and for others grows. What if honouring our vulnerability reminds us we are not alone; and that together we are powerful beyond measure?

9

What if...helping ourselves helps others?

Sometimes we want to help the people in our lives who are struggling and suffering in some way. Understandably so. But it's always worth checking what underpins our motivation and desire to help. Sometimes, deep down, we want the people in our lives to be happy so that then we can relax. *Then*, we can stop worrying about them. *Then*, we can be happy. This inadvertently places a lot of pressure on them...ultimately, to make us happy!

What if...helping ourselves helps others? What if our sole (soul) purpose is to enjoy life? What if the most powerful way we can help is by allowing joy into our own lives, regardless of how other people are feeling? Sound selfish? It is certainly a belief we have had impressed upon us, but is it valid? In truth, which is more selfish — wanting people to make us happy or inspiring other people to be happy?

10

*What if...*changing one habit today can change the course of our life?

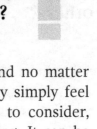

Sometimes we get a little stuck in life and no matter how desperately we want change, we may simply feel out of our depth. With so many things to consider, just thinking about it can be overwhelming. It can be difficult to know which way to turn. Where to start. But what if we don't have to change it all at once? What if we can simply make small changes? One at a time. Noticing what happens.

*What if...*changing one habit today can change the course of our life? Whether it be the decision to have a cup of tea rather than coffee, take a right turn instead of a left, to take a day off, not in sickness but in health. What if deciding differently today can shift our life in miraculous ways? That simple change of drink might stimulate a different thought pattern. In taking that right turn, we might bump into someone who brightens our day, or our life. A day off spent in joy might help us appreciate our work more, or indeed inspire us to change our work completely. In changing one habit, large or small, we are going from the familiar into the unknown. And as scary as this can feel, what if this is where the magic happens?

11

*What if...*stillness is healing?

Busyness can sometimes be a distraction that keeps us from addressing what we're really feeling. However, what isn't addressed emotionally tends to express itself in the body instead, through illness, pain and lethargy. It's tempting when feeling sick or tired to reach for externals to pep oneself up, to push on through, but what if this a false economy?

*What if...*stillness is healing? Taking a guilt-free rest, entering into a meditative state, or simply pausing where we are. At first, choosing stillness can go one of two ways. We may feel the immediate relief of allowing ourselves to stop, or we may feel quite uncomfortable. Usually in the form of intense boredom or irritation. This restlessness often occurs because in the stillness we are more able to feel our pain. Not just the physical, but the emotional pain driving the physical discomfort. It does take courage to be still. To feel it all. Yet, what if the resulting clarity, peace and joy makes it all worthwhile?

12

*What if...*we don't always need to know why?

When going through challenging times, we often feel better when we have a sense of why. Otherwise, we can find ourselves going round and round in circles. Trying to analyse and understand why this is happening, how we got into this 'mess', and what we can do about it. With such phrenetic activity, it's no wonder headaches and migraines exist!

*What if...*we don't always need to know why? What if, in moments like this, it's possible to simply accept what we are experiencing? Honour it. Be grateful for it. Even though we have no idea why. Choosing to trust that it is in our highest good. That if it's in our best interests to understand the details, all will be revealed in divine timing. What if, in this way, it is possible to experience a core of inner peace, no matter what is happening externally?

13

*What if...*there are no problems unless we create them?

Problem-solving can sometimes feel like a full-time job. *How are we going to make our money last the month? How do I deal with that tricky relationship? This illness? And how on earth are we going to achieve world peace?!* Yet what if problems only manifest if we focus on them? Individually and collectively.

*What if...*there are no problems unless we create them? Imagine then, there were no wars to fight, no people to heal, no poverty or hunger. With all the extra time on our hands, how would we choose to spend it? Painting, playing music, dancing, chatting with friends, travelling, going for walks, sky-diving, climbing mountains, laughing, singing, writing stories or poetry, tending the garden, growing our own food, hula-hooping, cooking delicious meals from scratch? The list of possibilities is infinite. What if we choose to live from this place of joy anyway? Lead the way.

14

*What if...*life is meant to be easy?

Many of us are raised to believe we don't get anywhere without hard work. Without pushing ourselves to the limit. *No pain, no gain!* Endlessly proving ourselves. Our worth. To be to the contrary is generally judged as being lazy. And yet, the hardest taskmaster and severest critic is often the voice within. But what if life doesn't have to be so tough?

*What if...*life is meant to be easy? What if, by easing up on ourselves and choosing what we want to do for the sheer delight of it, we accomplish just as much? Perhaps more. Yet, it doesn't feel *hard* and it doesn't feel like *work?* What if, in choosing to follow our joy, whether it be creating a masterpiece, creating jobs, creating an end to world poverty or creating fresh laundry, we move through it with greater ease and grace. Open to the possibility that perhaps life is meant to be ease-y after all.

15

*What if...*life isn't as random as it seems?

Extreme events, of both a personal and a global nature, can often leave us in a state of emotional turmoil. Seemingly making very little sense to us at the time. Which, in itself, can add to the anxiety. But what if, way beyond our individual lives, there is a benevolent order to it all? What if trying to control it all only interferes with the greater perfection?

*What if...*life isn't as random as it seems? When we cultivate a sense of inner peace, the natural rhythms, cycles and patterns of life tend to become more apparent. From the most fleeting, such as the inhale and exhale of the breath, to the billions of years it takes for stars to form and collapse back into formlessness. The cycle of birth, death and rebirth revealing itself over and over again. Kindly reminding us that for everything, there is both a rhyme and a reason.

16

*What if...*there are enough hours in the day?

Some may claim to thrive on adrenalin but generally speaking, feeling rushed, pressured and squeezed isn't a very pleasant experience. Playing an endless round of catch up can also take a toll on our health. The quicker we try to get it all done, the quicker time seems to pass. At the end of the day, we're often physically, mentally and emotionally drained. It is said that time is an illusion. On days like this, it's hard to imagine.

*What if...*there are enough hours in the day? What difference would it make to our experience? We might begin the day more at ease. Appreciate the weather. Sense the best way to nourish ourselves, thereby creating optimum energy. We might feel the urge to stretch a little, go for a walk or sit and just *be* for a while. Grateful for the unlimited time and space available right now. With our thinking mind calmed, there may be a sense of clarity. We might notice some tasks aren't that urgent after all. As for the things we would still like to accomplish, there may be a sense of lightness and joy. Effortless efficiency. Perhaps we'll sleep with a smile on our face tonight. Looking forward to another day with more than enough hours.

17

*What if...*we don't have to figure it all out?

Life can feel mentally exhausting at times. Trying to figure out the best food to eat, exercise to do, career to choose, time to start a family, words to use, and on and on and on. With such mental gymnastics going on, it's no wonder we're often physically tired too.

*What if...*we don't have to figure it all out? What if there is a divinely orchestrated flow to life? What if 'the best' is always going to be our experience if we surrender and allow ourselves to be carried along by it? Just like Marlin the clownfish in the film *Finding Nemo*. When, with great courage, he no longer resists the current but rather allows himself to be swept along by it. Ending up exactly where he wanted to be. Only much quicker, with far less effort, and some wonderful adventures along the way.

18

*What if...*being here is enough?

Many of us want to feel like we're making a difference in the world, whether for our own sake, for others, humanity, or the planet itself. For example, we may choose to become a musician, a counsellor, an aid worker, a forest ranger, or a multitude of other occupations in the hope that what we are doing will make a difference. For some, life can feel like one long search for meaning. Our *raison d'être*.

*What if...*being here is enough? What if simply by choosing to be born at this time, we are making all the difference in the world in a million ways we do not see from our individual perspective? Thereby free to do whatever we choose simply because our heart is in it. Because we enjoy it. Which, in turn, makes the world a more joyful place for all. Whether that's becoming a doctor, a street cleaner, an artist or a nun. Trusting that, however we choose to occupy ourselves, we are making a difference simply by being here.

19

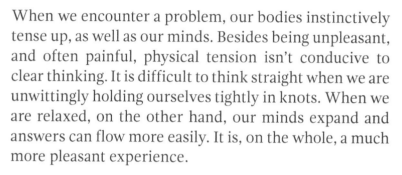

*What if...*relaxation is key?

When we encounter a problem, our bodies instinctively tense up, as well as our minds. Besides being unpleasant, and often painful, physical tension isn't conducive to clear thinking. It is difficult to think straight when we are unwittingly holding ourselves tightly in knots. When we are relaxed, on the other hand, our minds expand and answers can flow more easily. It is, on the whole, a much more pleasant experience.

*What if...*relaxation is key? In times of trouble, rather than trying to figure out the solution, what if, we first remember to let go of the physical tension? Doing whatever it is that helps our muscles to relax. In this moment. Noticing our breath. Stepping out into nature. Having a stretch. Taking a nap. Whatever works for us. And in doing so, opening ourselves up and allowing inspiration to arise with ease.

20

*What if...*being selfish isn't selfish after all?

Taking care of ourselves, *looking after number one*, can sometimes feel like a selfish act. Shameful, even. It's what many of us have been taught to believe by parents, schools, churches, and those who govern us. We've also been told by that same society that we must take personal responsibility. It can be very confusing. Do we look out for ourselves or not?

*What if...*being selfish isn't selfish after all? What if, by tending to our own needs, we *are* being responsible? And, in the process, no longer expecting others to solve our problems, shoulder the blame, or carry us. What if in letting go of any guilt or shame we might feel around looking after ourselves, being 'selfish' becomes a gift? Noticing that as we become less of a burden to others, we automatically inspire others to do the same simply by modelling how helping ourselves can help the Whole.

21

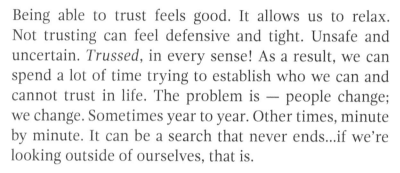

*What if...*the only person we need to trust is ourselves?

Being able to trust feels good. It allows us to relax. Not trusting can feel defensive and tight. Unsafe and uncertain. *Trussed*, in every sense! As a result, we can spend a lot of time trying to establish who we can and cannot trust in life. The problem is — people change; we change. Sometimes year to year. Other times, minute by minute. It can be a search that never ends...if we're looking outside of ourselves, that is.

*What if...*the only person we really need to trust is ourselves? Not necessarily trusting that we'll always do the right thing or make the best choices, but that we'll love ourselves whatever. Deeply. That we'll be honest with ourselves. Listen to ourselves with a kind ear. That, first and foremost, we'll be our own best friend. This doesn't mean we won't be loved and supported by others too. It simply means we'll be free to love ourselves and others, regardless.

22

*What if...*we are already free?

At times, there may appear to be very little freedom in our lives. We might feel trapped by external circumstances. As if there is nothing we can do. That our hands are tied behind our backs. Often we feel we have no choice, when in fact we do. It's just that the alternatives can feel too challenging or impossibly scary.

*What if...*we are already free? What if freedom isn't about external circumstances, but rather about how we choose to perceive those external circumstances? A state of mind. What if, by acknowledging the choices we do have (however unlikely we are to choose them), something loosens within us? Allows us to see life isn't simply black or white, but a whole rainbow of colour in between. That there is always an infinite spectrum of choice. What if, by appreciating choice exists, we begin to sense our inherent freedom?

23

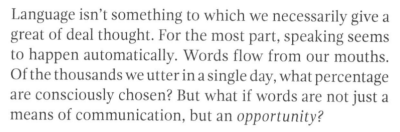

*What if...*our words create our reality?

Language isn't something to which we necessarily give a great of deal thought. For the most part, speaking seems to happen automatically. Words flow from our mouths. Of the thousands we utter in a single day, what percentage are consciously chosen? But what if words are not just a means of communication, but an *opportunity*?

*What if...*our words create our reality? Not in isolation, of course. Many factors influence our experience of life, but what if the language we use is reflected back to us? Whatever we voice continually becoming our experience. How would this alter the way we choose to express ourselves? What if, for example, when we say *That'll never work!* or *I'm such an idiot!* it becomes our experience? What reality would we prefer to talk ourselves into? In this case, choosing the words *This is sure to work!* and *I am a powerful creator!* could, quite literally, make a world of difference.

24

What if... we are a unique piece of the cosmic puzzle?

Life can feel like a complete mystery at times, and we may find ourselves looking to others for clues. It can seem as if everybody else has the answers, except us. Like we're missing something.

What if... we are a unique piece of the cosmic puzzle? Our joy being the missing piece. What if, by allowing ourselves to follow our joy, and others theirs, we are playing our part? Lighting up ourselves and the planet in our own particular way. What if, by having the courage to add our little piece of the puzzle to the great mystery of life, the bigger picture forms before our eyes?

25

*What if...*our pain is here to help?

It's understandable that as soon as we feel any pain, we want it to stop. Sometimes we can feel so tense and hold ourselves so rigidly around our pain that we unwittingly make it worse. But what if the pain is a message?

*What if...*our pain is here to help? Encouraging us to take better care of ourselves. What if, by ignoring, numbing or distracting ourselves from it, we miss its benevolence? Repeat the behaviour. And hence the pain returns. Intensifying over time from a whisper, to a shout, to a full-blown scream. What if, by responding to pain with a moment of quiet, still, surrender, we get to hear the message? Perhaps the cut on our thumb is telling us things are far from 'thumbs up'! Could that itchy rash be reflecting unexpressed irritation? Or are we secretly regretting a *rash* decision? Maybe that back injury is insisting we get the *back up* we need. What if, once we hear the message and take care of ourselves accordingly, the pain no longer needs to be here?

26

*What if...*the perfect pace is our own?

We can sometimes feel pressured around the pace at which we are moving through life. Especially if we have a tendency to look around and compare ourselves to others. Are we going too slow? Are we going too fast? The term *human race* can feel quite apt!

*What if...*the perfect pace is our own? What if the challenge, should there be any, is to discover, enjoy, and be at peace with our own pace? To appreciate our journey whatever we perceive our progress to be. And besides, what are we expecting once we cross the finish line?

27

What if...we simply see what unfolds?

Keeping tight control of our lives may seem like ultimate efficiency and if we are really enjoying the process, then great! However, what often lies beneath our desire to control is fear. The physical manifestation of which is tension, usually leading to some degree of pain. Whether that be a mild stomach ache or a full-blown chronic illness. But what if we don't have to make ourselves ill trying to assure our future?

What if...we simply see what unfolds? Physically relax. Mentally relax. Breathe. And allow. A scary thought, perhaps. Irresponsible, even. Surrendering control and trusting that Life has our back. Has it all in hand in the most perfect way while we get on with the business of enjoying our everyday lives. Loving ourselves. Loving one another. I guess we won't know unless we try.

28

*What if...*our anger is an opportunity for peace?

Lashing out in anger, whether verbally or physically, may bring us a nanosecond of relief, but if inner peace is our goal, being angry can feel dreadful. Immense guilt and shame may ensue, causing us to repress the anger. Pushing it back down into the dark recesses from where it came. Waiting to rise again when we least expect it.

*What if...*our anger is an opportunity for peace? What if, by acknowledging and exploring our anger, we are able to identify the root cause? What if, when we trace it back far enough and often enough, we realise we are really only ever angry with ourselves? Angry for what we did or didn't do. Did or didn't say. Angry for allowing ourselves to be spun in the same old circles. Backed into the same old corner. What if our anger is trying to protect us? Set us free. What if we simply need to hear what it is saying? How it is insisting we look after ourselves. Thereby giving us the power to release it.

29

What if...simplicity is key to joy?

Despite the adage *less is more*, unless we disconnect ourselves technologically from time to time, it's quite easy to be seduced by the bombardment of advertising coming at us 24/7, urging us to buy more, have more, be more. Society at large tends to support this idea in that the more we amass, the more we seem to be revered. Not that there is anything intrinsically wrong with how much we have; the question is — are we any happier for it?

What if...simplicity is key to joy? Letting go of unwanted and unnecessary items can bring a delightful sense of relief. A lightening of the load, as it were. The more we have, the more energy we need to invest in maintaining it. It can be exhausting. Which in turn can take a toll on our health. But what if the power of the decluttering process lies not just in our physical possessions, but in our minds? What if, in letting go of those things that drain us — possessions, thoughts, beliefs, relationships and habits alike — our energy naturally increases? We become revitalised. Healthier. Happier. Free to simply enjoy life.

30

*What if...*we're having exactly the experience we need?

Life doesn't always seem to go our way. It doesn't always feel pleasant. In fact, it can be pretty painful at times. Especially when we're not consciously creating it. When we are on *autopilot*, as it were. Mindlessly *going through the motions*. In a trance. Creating unconsciously through our fears. Although we might not be having the experience we want...

*What if...*we're having exactly the experience we need? Each situation a chance to enlighten ourselves a little more. About ourselves and the world around us. An opportunity to release our fears. To liberate ourselves. To lighten up. And, as our fears diminish, to experience greater love. A trance-formation worth experiencing!

31

*What if...*the most dangerous terrorist is within?

Switching on a news channel any time of day or night, one can find reports of terrorism. A constant stream of fearful images suggesting we should be afraid. Very afraid! Outraged, even. Up in arms. Literally. Urging us to war. But what if the outside world isn't the source of the problem? Nor the solution.

*What if...*the most dangerous terrorist is within? How often do we *beat ourselves up* with guilt and shame? Torture ourselves with regret? Set ourselves *punishingly* high standards. And then *judge* and *criticise* ourselves for not living up to them. Unwittingly, holding others *hostage* to those same impossibly high expectations. The good news is, if we are our *own worst enemy*, then we also have the power to change it. To stop terrorising ourselves. Practise a little self-love instead. Creating a kinder and more loving world in the process.

32

What if...feeling bad is good?

When feeling bad about something, we often distract or numb ourselves from the discomfort. It's understandable. After all, who wants to feel bad? We may fear if we were to stop and feel our 'badness', even for a moment, we might fall into an endless pit of despair. So, we continue keeping busy, busy. Anything to avoid feeling what we're feeling.

What if...feeling bad is good? What if it's an opportunity to stop and listen to ourselves. Gain a little clarity. Address what's not okay for us right now? In giving ourselves the time and space to feel our 'badness' without judgement, we might even begin to notice the *silver lining* around the situation. The *blessing in disguise*. Enabling us to move through the 'badness' and out the other side. To a place where we can breathe and feel good again. Perhaps feeling bad isn't so bad after all.

33

*What if...*money flows in and out as easily as we breathe in and out?

We may feel a lot of pressure around money. Earning it, spending it, saving it. Particularly when it is scarce. Though even an abundance of money can come with its own peculiar pressures. *How do I maintain this? Should I be sharing this? How much? With whom?* Either way, it can feel like being on a hamster wheel at times. Never-ending. Unless, of course, we get off. What if relaxing around money actually brings forth more?

*What if...*money flows in and out as easily as we breathe in and out? Our breath an indicator of flow. Our current state of being. What if all the stress we feel around money (or anything else, for that matter) prevents it coming into our lives? Or at least limits our enjoyment and appreciation of it when it does. What if breathing deep and easy helps us tap into all the ways in which we are already abundant — with or without money? What if tapping into this *current of appreciation* allows *currency to appreciate* in our lives?

34

What if...the purpose of relationship is growth?

Love is often thought to be the point of relationship, but what does this mean exactly? We often have (or have been sold) culturally preconceived ideas of love. In the West, for example, meeting the perfect partner and living happily ever after. Nice idea but an immense amount of pressure and not necessarily much fun in reality!

What if...the purpose of relationship is growth? Okay, not as romantic at first glance, but what if growth is the purpose of *all* relationships? Romantic or otherwise. Particularly those with whom we struggle. Whether it be a lover, friend, family member or stranger, what if being in relationship with another gives us an ongoing opportunity to develop a deeper understanding of ourselves? In relation to one another. As mirrors reflecting each other. Being open to the possibility that when we feel hurt or angered by someone (or any other feeling), perhaps they are feeling exactly the same about us. That maybe this issue is coming up between us to allow us both the opportunity to process and release it? What if, in repeatedly freeing ourselves this way, we find ourselves naturally in love with ourselves and each other?

35

*What if...*the internet is a reflection of our natural ability to connect?

Love it or loathe it, the creation of the internet is certainly bringing us the opportunity to connect and communicate with more people, more quickly, more of the time. A message that once would have taken weeks by ship to travel from one continent to another can now be conveyed in an instant. But what if we've always had the ability to communicate with anyone, anywhere, any time? Throughout the ages, people have spoken of our inherent, if dormant, telepathic abilities (and were possibly burned at the stake for doing so!) Nowadays, there is a whole branch of science, and Government, dedicated to the exploration of such matters.

*What if...*the internet is a reflection of our natural ability to connect? Our capacity to communicate with each other over vast distances without the aid of external devices. Sensing the presence of another through quietening the mind and going within. Being open to the possibility and allowing *ourselves* to go online, as it were. It would certainly be handy should the internet ever go down!

36

What if...peace on earth already exists?

Crazy one, right? *Have you seen the state of the world?!* one might justifiably retort. Yes, there does appear to be a lot of hostility on the planet. Prejudice, inequality, suffering. It's all going on! Never mind the personal battles we're fighting at home and within ourselves. But what if, amid all this warring, it's still possible to experience peace on earth? Right where we are.

What if...peace on earth already exists? That regardless of how external circumstances might appear, we are always free to attune ourselves to it. However outrageous it might seem. What if, in having the courage to allow ourselves to experience a sense of inner peace in our daily lives, rather than being selfish, naïve or downright delusional, as some might suggest, we are active in creating a more peaceful reality? Not just for ourselves, but humanity as a whole. Literally *being light* in the darkness. Choosing peace and staying here, in the present moment, until the whole world joins us. One-by-one. Being the peace we wish to see in the world.

37

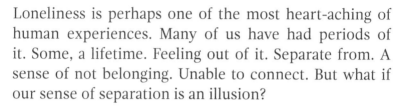

*What if...*we are never truly alone?

Loneliness is perhaps one of the most heart-aching of human experiences. Many of us have had periods of it. Some, a lifetime. Feeling out of it. Separate from. A sense of not belonging. Unable to connect. But what if our sense of separation is an illusion?

*What if...*we are never truly alone? What if there is a vast amount of love and support around us, but we simply don't see it? Whether that be a friend or family member, who is unsure of how to help us in our plight, but loves us anyway. Whether it's a community support group that is there especially for people like us — but alas we do not recognise it. Whether it be individuals around the world. People just like us. Wanting exactly what we want. A sense of connection. A better and friendlier world for everyone. What if we are loved in infinite ways that we simply cannot comprehend right now?

38

*What if...*it's possible to see clearly before the rain has gone?

Everyone experiences stormy periods occasionally. For some, it may be more frequent. Whether physical, mental, emotional, or spiritual in nature, it can be a confusing time. Often our tendency is to *batten down the hatches*. Get our heads down and anxiously *weather the storm*. Good nautical advice! But what if, rather than waiting for the storm to pass, it's possible to appreciate it while we're in it?

*What if...*it's possible to see clearly before the rain has gone? To notice it's okay to relax *during* the storm. To trust that whatever is happening is absolutely in our best interests, however unlikely it may seem in the moment. However unfathomable it is. What if the storm is here to challenge and clear old habits, patterns, behaviours and beliefs that are no longer working for us? What if in remembering, even on the stormiest of days, that the sun is still shining behind the clouds, we aid our own swift return to health and happiness. Making way for a brighter day.

39

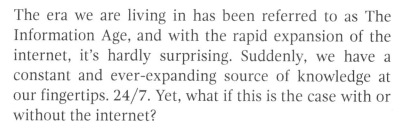

*What if...*everything is information?

The era we are living in has been referred to as The Information Age, and with the rapid expansion of the internet, it's hardly surprising. Suddenly, we have a constant and ever-expanding source of knowledge at our fingertips. 24/7. Yet, what if this is the case with or without the internet?

*What if...*everything is information? Life itself, a metaphor. Continually reflecting us back to ourselves in infinite ways. Through colour, the weather, our choice of food, the clothes we wear, the state of our house, our car, our relationships, and even the content of our dreams. Does the torrent of rain reflect the tears we feel like crying? Or the clear blue sky mirror the clarity and expansiveness we feel today. Does the state of our loft equate to the state of our mind? Is that dream of falling encouraging us to take a leap of faith? Or the dream about flying urging us to let go and soar with our personal dreams and aspirations? What if, through metaphor, life is continually informing us of who we are? Life infinitely communicating with Itself.

40

*What if...*we stop putting off happiness until...?

Whether we are focused on a daily to-do list or a lifetime ambition, it's tempting to think *I'll just do this and then I'll relax.* Or, *Once I've achieved that, I'll be happy.* Nice theory, except what often happens is, once we've ticked an item off the list, something else takes its place. In fact, the to-do list never actually ends. Similarly, once the initial elation of achieving an ambition wears off, we may start looking for the next big thing we think will make us happy. It can have us going round and round in circles. Chasing happiness and never quite arriving.

*What if...*we stop putting off happiness until...? What if we choose happiness right here and now, whatever we are doing. It doesn't necessarily mean having no to-do list, but noticing the joy available in the process. No matter how mundane the items. Washing dishes, paying taxes, grocery shopping, you name it, it can all be enjoyed and appreciated if we choose. We can still achieve whatever we want to — only happiness is no longer the destination. It's the whole journey!

41

*What if...*our sense of contraction and expansion is guiding us?

With so many decisions and choices to be made, and with so much (often conflicting) advice and information coming our way, it's no wonder we often feel lost and confused when trying to navigate life. But what if we are able to simplify our decision-making process? Make it a little more black and white.

*What if...*our sense of contraction and expansion is guiding us? When faced with a choice, what if, by bringing gentle awareness to our body, we begin to notice whether it is contracting or expanding? Tense or relaxed. Fearful or loving. Using this to orient us toward a more joyful existence. Simple. Black and white. Choosing whether to be guided by fear or love.

42

*What if...*lovingly observing ourselves is funny?

When life is feeling too serious, it's worth taking a little time to simply observe ourselves. Doing whatever it is we do. Our patterns and habits. Our typical behaviour. Watching the way we tie ourselves in knots, back ourselves into corners, and spin ourselves round in circles. When we lovingly observe ourselves for long enough, we often start to see the funny side of life.

*What if...*lovingly observing ourselves is funny? Amid the proliferation of shorthand texting and messaging, the abbreviation LOL (Laugh Out Loud) is perhaps one of the more popular. It's funny then, the act of repeatedly loving and observing ourselves; Love. Observe. Love. Observe. Love. Observe. Love. Observe. Love... becomes abbreviated to a never-ending sequence of LOL!

43

*What if...*treating ourselves is sometimes mis-treating ourselves?

Who doesn't like a treat?! Whether it's as luxurious as a holiday, or as simple as a glass of wine at the end of a busy day, it feels wonderful to reward ourselves now and again. There's no doubt about it — we all deserve to feel good. To value ourselves. To celebrate. So why is it, once the initial high is over, we don't necessarily feel good in the long term?

*What if...*treating ourselves is sometimes mis-treating ourselves? Well-intentioned, perhaps, but not so helpful in the long run. Not necessarily the treat itself, but judging it as so. It can be a great motivator but, in labelling something 'a treat' we are often unwittingly attaching a judgement of deserving or not deserving to it. To ourselves, essentially! Not so much of a problem when we deem ourselves to be performing in a way that feels worthy, but what about the rest of the time? Most of the time! There can be a tendency to either deny ourselves or to treat ourselves anyway — and feel bad either way. Yet, what if we are always worthy? *How will I ever motivate myself to do anything?* we may protest. What if, by allowing ourselves to be inspired into action through worthiness, everything becomes a treat?

44

What if...ultimately, there is nothing we need to learn?

What we know, how much we can learn, how many facts and figures we can readily recite, how many qualifications we have, whether we are capable of producing results — these are all things our society tends to value highly. This is how we have become used to proving ourselves. Our worth. And it starts at a very young age. As wonderful as a sense of achievement can be, the pressure we often feel under to accomplish more and more can be so immense, our health and happiness begin to suffer. Pursuing the very things we hope will increase it!

What if...ultimately, there is nothing we need to learn? To be whole. Complete. What if we simply are these things already? Free to achieve anything we desire without attaching our sense of self-worth to it. No need to qualify or justify our place in this world. Realising we are valuable, precious, and worthy, regardless of our attainments. What if life is a natural process of gathering information — only for us to ultimately let go of it? Realising it is not so much what we know in our heads, but what we truly know within our hearts, that creates our health and happiness.

45

*What if...*we don't have to complete a *What if...?* question right now?

Although a sense of structure and routine can be helpful in life, it can also feel restrictive at times. As if, the more we try to stick to it, the harder it becomes. On these occasions, simply noticing our resistance can be most transformative...and curiously productive!

*What if...*we don't have to complete a *What if...?* question right now? Allowing the resistance to be here. Breathing. Creating space. What if, in bringing gentle awareness to the truth of how we are feeling, without the need to do anything about it, something softens? The answer arises in response to the question. Through surrender, the *What if...?* question essentially writes itself!

46

*What if...*we are what we seek?

Searching can be a lot of fun. A thrill, in fact. 'Not finding' can be frustrating. Depressing, even. Often what we desire (clarity, connection, perfection, freedom, love, or anything else), we tend to seek outside ourselves. Through other people, other places, outer experiences. But what if all these qualities are within us?

*What if...*we are what we seek? Making *self-realisation* the ultimate thrill! *Remembrance* the ultimate goal. That all we desire is within us. Still free to enjoy the world and all life has to offer. Yet, coming from a place of already being content. Already connected. Already here. What if we have been hiding from ourselves all along? What if we are the love we seek?

47

*What if...*life is on our side?

At times it might feel like the world is against us. A harsh, hostile, and unforgiving place. But what if this is a reflection of how we are feeling deep inside? How we are unwittingly treating ourselves. Rather than life resisting us, what if it is us who are resisting life?

*What if...*life is on our side? Encouraging us. Our best friend. What if, by simply *noticing what we notice* as we go through daily life, we are able to connect with this constant source of support? Get a sense of what is really going on with us. Brakes gone on our car? Are we unwittingly *on overdrive?* Biting our nails to the bone? Are we judgementally *eating away at ourselves?* Wearing that padded gilet like a bulletproof vest? Perhaps we are feeling *shot at* from all directions. Or *bombarded* with bullets of self-criticism! What if, then, the challenges we encounter are life gently guiding us back to where we really want to be? In love with Life.

48

What if...colour can help us?

What is it about a rainbow that tends to lift our spirit? Despite the often ominous presence of rain clouds in the distance! When our own lives are gloomy, or even downright stormy, there are any number of support systems we may turn toward for guidance. Family. A good friend, perhaps. A therapist. A doctor. The Church. The list of ways in which we might lighten up is infinite.

*What if...*colour can help us? Whether it be the colour of our environment, the colour of the clothes we choose to wear, or the foods we choose to eat. As a frequency of light, what if colour can be used to attune ourselves to a particular vibration? A *vibe*, as it were. The Chakra system purports that each colour on the spectrum promotes certain qualities within us. What if, by wearing, decorating, consuming or simply focusing on any given colour, we can harness its power for our own wellbeing? Perhaps rainbows are so uplifting because they encompass the whole spectrum. Reminding us of our own innate completeness.

49

*What if...*there's plenty for everybody?

Resources do appear to be limited on this planet and the distribution of wealth is certainly unequal. It's no wonder then that competition is a strong feature of our society, with a drive to amass our own personal fortune and then to protect it. Also known as being in *survival mode*. But what if it's possible to experience abundance without having to strive and drive and push?

What if...there's plenty for everybody? Noticing that nature constantly provides humanity with everything we can possibly need. Naturally replenishing itself. Over and over. A steady source of abundance. No need to compare, amass or protect. Leaving us free to fully enjoy its ever-ripening fruits. What if, from this place of inherent freedom and prosperity, creating, building and thriving becomes immense fun? Knowing, either way, we are contributing heartily.

50

*What if...*time didn't exist before we measured it?

Since humans created the measurement of time (seconds, minutes, hours, days, months, years, millennia and so on) did time exist before we labeled and defined it? Did we create the concept? Scientists have shown that an experiment is affected by the presence of the experimenter (an observer). Were we to suddenly stop observing time, then, would it alter our experience of it? Would it cease to exist altogether?

*What if...*time didn't exist before we measured it? Imagining it is tricky enough, but speaking of it takes a whole shift in consciousness. For example, the original question *What if time didn't exist before we measured it?* itself becomes redundant. If time doesn't exist, there is no before! Besides, why would we even choose to consider such a peculiar possibility? It's true that having a sense of time can help us navigate life, but it can also be restrictive. We are forever running out of it, and it often seems to be going too fast or too slow for comfort. What if, in letting go of time as we know it, we liberate ourselves a little? We are no longer a slave to it. In fact, if time doesn't exist, then can we ever truly begin or end? Even the words *eternal*, *everlasting*, and *always* are references to time. So, could it be that we simply *are*?

51

*What if...*we are complete?

There's no doubt a sense of completion is a wonderful feeling, yet we often place immense pressure on ourselves to see all manner of things through to the end. *Push, push, push!* It can be quite a punishing process at times. Including a great deal of guilt and shame around leaving things unfinished and undone. But how much joy are we experiencing along the way?

*What if...*we are complete? Often behind the desire to do, achieve and create, is a deep-seated fear that we are not enough. That we must prove ourselves. Our worth. Even to ourselves. Yet, what if the only reason to do, achieve and create anything is simply for the fun of it? The pure joy. What if an uncompleted goal does not make us any less whole?

52

*What if...*we are already fulfilling our purpose?

Many of us are searching for a greater sense of meaning in our life. Trying to figure out our purpose, as it were. Our reason for being here. It can be rather a costly business in terms of time, energy and money spent. Still, we can feel as if we are getting nowhere fast! Going round in circles, even.

*What if...*we are already fulfilling our purpose? Simply by showing up. Choosing to be born a uniquely individual part of this shared experience called Life. What if, even if we feel we aren't participating or contributing in any way, we are? Simply with our presence. Nothing to find, nothing to prove. This would free us to do the things that light us up. Enjoy ourselves. Perhaps even lighting up the world as we go along. Now *this* feels like a sense of purpose!

53

*What if...*Planet Earth is alive?

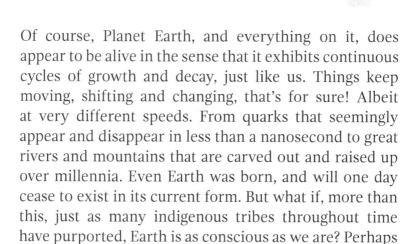

Of course, Planet Earth, and everything on it, does appear to be alive in the sense that it exhibits continuous cycles of growth and decay, just like us. Things keep moving, shifting and changing, that's for sure! Albeit at very different speeds. From quarks that seemingly appear and disappear in less than a nanosecond to great rivers and mountains that are carved out and raised up over millennia. Even Earth was born, and will one day cease to exist in its current form. But what if, more than this, just as many indigenous tribes throughout time have purported, Earth is as conscious as we are? Perhaps more so!

*What if...*Planet Earth is alive? Okay, for most of us a planet is not what we are inclined to think of as a conscious being. We humans tend to be, on the whole, quite self-limiting when it comes to what we are willing to accept or recognise as other intelligent life forms. But what if, in truth, we are able to connect and communicate with Planet Earth? Support each other. Imagine having Mother Earth on our side as we journey through space together. What a stellar travelling companion!

54

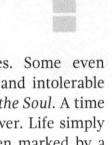

*What if...*we are here to lighten up?

Life can feel pretty intense at times. Some even experience a period of great darkness and intolerable anguish referred to as the *Dark Night of the Soul*. A time when one feels one cannot sink any lower. Life simply could not be any worse than it is. Often marked by a deep sense of depression, confusion and loss. We have *hit rock bottom*. A scary time indeed! But what if this is all part of the transformational process?

*What if...*we are here to lighten up? To find our way through the dark. As terrifying as it may seem, what if there is health in allowing ourselves to sink to our lowest? To get in touch with our perceived sense of darkness within. What if it's only in surrendering to it that we see it for the illusion it is, and begin to rise back up again like the proverbial phoenix from the ashes? Wiser and lighter than before. What if we experience this process at a collective level too? That as humanity lightens up individually, the whole planet becomes a lighter, brighter and more loving place to be? What if this is what enlightenment really is? A return to our natural state of *light, being*.

55

*What if...*gentleness is our strength?

There is often an assumption that to get things moving, whether it be a situation, another person, or ourselves, we need to apply force. That unless we push things along, nothing will ever get done. It can create a lot of friction, literally! Physically, mentally and emotionally. Our health can suffer as well as our peace of mind. But what if, whatever is in our highest interest happens anyway, whether we force it or not?

*What if...*gentleness is our strength? No need to wear ourselves out. Drain ourselves. What if applying kindness to a situation, to ourselves, allows a gentle flow to take us where we need to be? It might take longer. It might not. But either way, the journey is guaranteed to be a delightful one.

56

*What if...*illness is an opportunity?

Perhaps it's human nature that when we are experiencing illness, when we are feeling pain, there is an urge to be rid of it as quickly as possible. A *no-brainer* really. Who would choose to be in pain, right? To suffer.

*What if...*illness is an opportunity? Not to suggest we go looking for it. Wish for it. Bring it on. But when it is here, when we are in the midst of it anyway, what if there's a chance to learn something about ourselves? Discovering a way through the pain by acknowledging its emotional counterpart. In allowing ourselves a moment of non-resistance to it, we might realise our difficulty in swallowing reflects the feeling we have about an unwanted situation. That our earache is suggesting we listen. To ourselves, perhaps. And so on. What if, in this way, it's possible to turn pain and suffering into wisdom? Trusting there is a greater reason for it. Noticing that when we soften into and acknowledge the emotional pain, even for the briefest of moments, the physical pain often dissipates.

57

*What if...*eating is optional?

Eating can be such a pleasure. A real delight. However, with so much pressure around body image, as well as conflicting advice around health and fitness in general, the resulting tension we often feel around food can take the joy right out of it. Moreover, many of us eat not only to survive, but unwittingly use food as a coping mechanism. To cheer ourselves up. To be social. To dull the lonely ache in our stomach. To celebrate. To medicate. The list goes on.

*What if...*eating is optional? The belief that we need food to survive is so strong, any suggestion otherwise may seem like an utterly ridiculous notion. Some may even call it dangerous and irresponsible. Yet, people throughout history have claimed not only to survive, but thrive, on fresh air, sunshine and water. So, what if we are only as dependent on food as we believe we are? What if, in detaching from a sense of *needing* food for survival or as a way to cope, we are left with the freedom to simply enjoy it?

58

What if...a single thought can change our reality?

When seeking transformation in our lives, whether it be leaving a relationship, pursuing a particular career, or simply desiring a more joyful daily experience, the amount of change we perceive we need to make in order to get to where we want to be can be overwhelming. It can put us off before we even begin. But what if thinking of *all* the changes is unnecessary?

What if...a single thought can change our reality? Set off a chain reaction that carries us effortlessly in the direction we want to head. Imagine we suddenly wonder *What if there is no right or wrong?* What if this simple (if a little crazy-seeming) thought somehow releases us from burdens and feelings of guilt and shame that are holding us back. Preventing us from making the changes we want to make. What if this single thought leads us to consider whether ultimately all that matters is what *we* perceive to be right or wrong for *us?* Whether we are in alignment with our own ethical point of view. Living out our own inner values. Perhaps, as a result, we begin to act differently. See the world through less judgemental eyes. In this way, we may experience for ourselves just how powerful and transformative a single thought can be.

59

What if...all paths lead home?

With so many belief systems in the world, so many filters through which to view life, trying to figure out *the* truth, knowing what and whom to believe, can feel mind-boggling at times. We might look through the various therapeutic, astrological, religious, cultural, political or scientific lenses, to name but a few. In fact, the list is so extensive, it's easy to become judgemental. Comparing our own beliefs with those of others. But what if such diversity isn't a problem?

What if...all paths lead home? No *right* or *best* way. No need to believe what we're told to believe, but free to follow whichever path we prefer. To view life through whichever lens we like. Whichever brings us the most joy and the greatest sense of connection. Knowing that the belief system itself isn't the truth, but merely a vehicle taking us there. Or rather, taking us Here. To the present moment. Home already.

60

What if...the key to freedom is surrender?

Life can sometimes feel like a battleground with us, *the troops*, dodging metaphorical bullets left, right and centre. Indeed, throughout our history there have been many wars fought. It's perhaps unsurprising then, when faced with tough situations, there can be a tendency for us to take up positions of defence and attack. To toughen up. Stand our ground. *Soldier on!* But what if there is an easier, more pleasurable way?

What if...the key to freedom is surrender? As counter-intuitive as it may seem in the midst of our own personal troubles, what if it's okay to relax? Soften. Open up. Take a breath. Take our time. Let the bullets fly right past us. Right through us even, and out the other side. Noticing their impact and yet seeing them for the illusion they really are. Simply bullets of fear flying back and forth.

61

*What if...*being both masculine and feminine is unifying?

From a biological perspective (with some exceptions), being a man or a woman seems pretty clear-cut. Moreover, the cultural roles and expectations that have been impressed and often imposed upon us, depending on our sex, have also been pretty well-defined over the ages. Yet, despite the social progress made, there is still great inequality between the sexes. We are still divided in many ways.

*What if...*being both masculine and feminine is unifying? One life energy expressing itself in two distinctly opposite ways. Two sides of the same coin. What if, then, our *true* power lies not in being male or female, but in combining, merging, reconnecting, and unifying both masculine and feminine energies within ourselves? How might we do this? Paradox! Being *compassionately direct. Fiercely loving.* A *gentle warrior.* Taking *inspired action.* Or any other combination of 'masculine' and 'feminine' energies one can think of. Could this be what marriage is really all about? Simply a metaphor of the union and the balance that is required to take place within so that we may experience our innate Wholeness.

62

*What if...*speaking in the present tense helps us stay present?

Despite our regrets of the past and fears about the future, over and over and over again, we are told the present is where we find all we desire. The truth of who we are. The trouble is, *being in the Now* can feel like trying to hold onto a wet fish. As elusive as it is simple-sounding! So how on earth do we manage it?

*What if...*speaking in the present tense helps us stay present? Our language, and more specifically the tense in which we choose to speak, helping anchor us in the Here and Now. Using *here* rather than *there, this* instead of *that*, and *am* rather than *will*. It can certainly take a bit of getting used to, but being mindful of where we are placing ourselves time-wise through the language we choose can be a real *gift*. Perhaps that...or rather *this* is why it's called the *present*!

63

*What if...*ageing is optional?

With the abundance of pricey lotions, potions, surgeries and interventions readily available these days, there is no doubt that *anti-ageing* is big business! But what if our physical experience of ageing has as much to do with our state of mind? Our beliefs and our fears around the ageing process. What if feeling stressed around ageing is ageing in itself?

*What if...*ageing is optional? Not necessarily in terms of numbers (as long as we're observing time and counting the years, we'll age numerically) but the *expectation* of deterioration and ill-health with age. How would we behave differently if we knew we could be healthy for the whole of our life? What if not feeling so *grave* about ageing is the anti-*gravity* (anti-*serious*), anti-ageing cure we seek!

64

What if... our body is a compass?

We might seek advice in a number of areas of life — health, morals, finances, and career to name but a few. More often than not, that guidance comes from an external source. From an expert. A guru. But what if we have our own internal guidance system? And what if the body is the instrument?

What if... our body is a compass? A wise body of intelligence. Pointing us in the best direction at all times. Way beyond our thinking mind. Yet, what if life is so noisy and busy for the most part, it's difficult to tune into? What if all we need do, then, is...nothing. Simply stilling and quietening ourselves from time to time. Enough to hear the whispers. Feel the gentle nudges this way and that. Noticing the signs. And letting ourselves be guided accordingly.

65

*What if...*both sexes suffer as a result of gender inequality?

For thousands of years now, humankind has lived in predominantly patriarchal societies. With the cultural rules, belief systems and general structure being dictated, for the most part, by masculine energy. (The fact that it is more often referred to as *mankind* being a prime example!) Such societies have tended to favour men and devalue women. Many women have suffered, and still are suffering, as a result of the inevitable gender inequality created.

*What if...*both sexes suffer as a result of gender inequality? It may seem as if men have all the power in patriarchal societies, but can men truly be happy in societies that undermine their own mothers, sisters and daughters? Moreover, not only have women been denied access to the incredible power of feminine energy, but men are denying themselves access too. Castrating themselves in the process. Denying themselves the experience of Wholeness. Unity. Love. Where true power lies. From this perspective, gender inequality is of no benefit to anyone.

66

What if...it's all b*ll*cks?

It seems the planet, humanity and we as individuals are going through a period of great change. A shift of global proportions. A perfect time to release any old, outdated belief systems that are no longer working for us, and instead embrace new beliefs that feel more in alignment with who we truly are. Many are consciously choosing a more heart-centred way of being. Both a liberating and incredibly vulnerable choice at times. In this ever-changing world, it can take great courage to walk our own path. Moments of doubt and sudden panic are, perhaps, unsurprising.

*What if...it's all b*ll*cks?!* When choosing to live from the heart, it's not uncommon to occasionally wonder *What if I'm wrong?! Deluding myself? Am I making a fool of myself?* Indeed, one may be judged as being *away with the fairies, in La-la land* and not *in the real world.* Such criticism may not just come from others, we may even fear it ourselves. What if it turns out that there is nothing beyond this life, that love isn't all there is, that we aren't all interconnected after all? What if we are wrong? Well...does it matter? Right or wrong, what a beautiful way to live.

67

*What if...*our thoughts determine our health?

We tend to make physical changes in order to change our physical health. If we want to alter our weight, for example, we might choose to work out. Sometimes, punishingly. Despite our best efforts, however, intentions frequently fall to the wayside. Leading to self-criticism. Yet, thinking badly of ourselves is often precisely what leads us to make unhealthy choices in the first place! So, what if it's possible to change our physical experience by altering our mental state?

*What if...*our thoughts determine our health? For better or worse. Our choice. What if thinking kindly of ourselves promotes not only our mental wellbeing, but our physical too? Inspiring us, perhaps, to exercise in ways that are more pleasurable and, therefore, sustainable. While reducing the urge to make poor health choices to begin with! As much as our thoughts can be detri*mental*, what if, depending on the ones we choose, they can also be the source of our health?

68

What if...our imagination is real?

When young, using our imagination often comes naturally through play. Pretending. Inventing. Dreaming. As we get older, however, we may be chastised for *living in a dream world*. As a result, using our own imagination as an adult can sometimes feel rather... naïve. Counterintuitive. Risky, even. The idiom *building castles in the air* springs to mind.

*What if...*our imagination is real? Everything we create in the physical world begins with a thought. An idea. What if our imagination, then, is the starting point of creation? Of course, action may still be required to physically manifest it. But what if the truth is we dream ourselves into reality? If we're free to imagine and create whatever we want, why not choose something wonderful? Something that makes the physical effort not only worth it, but a delight in itself.

69

*What if...*the songs we absent-mindedly sing or hum are a message?

Perhaps we've never given much thought to the tunes we hum or songs we absent-mindedly sing. We might assume we've simply heard it on the radio or picked it up from someone around us. The last song we heard. Nothing more.

*What if...*the songs we absent-mindedly sing or hum are a message? A glimpse of how we (or others) are really feeling. What if a particular lyric, or the overall theme of the song, is something our unconscious really wants us to know? A valuable insight. A little like Bumblebee in the *Transformers* movie. A car/robot that, having lost his voice, communicates through songs played through the car's radio. Sure, we may be simply repeating a song we've heard, but, on the other hand, it just might turn out to be a wonderful source of information.

70

What if... we're just playing at being human?

Life can feel so darn serious at times! An endless round of survival. Life and death, in fact. With so much battling in the world, and so much misery as a result, the thought of easing up, relaxing, playing even, can sometimes feel utterly irresponsible. But what if, ultimately, life itself is a game?

What if... we're just playing at being human? Choosing to be here to experience the turmoil that is happening on the planet right now. Just to see if we can remember — in the midst of these darkest and most painful of times — who we truly are. Light *playing* at being dark. If so, fancy co-creating something a little lighter?

71

*What if...*we R.I.P before dying?

Rest In Peace is a phrase we tend to reserve for those who have passed. It gives a sense of all the hard work of living being over. A wish that a soul finds eternal peace and rest in the afterlife. If there is an afterlife, are we really going to be eternally still? Or are there other experiences to explore? Either way, why put off being peaceful and restful now?

*What if...*we R.I.P. before dying? *Too busy,* we say. *Unrealistic. Boring,* even. True, life is often full, and many wouldn't consider resting in peace an option, but what if resting in peace doesn't necessarily mean doing nothing, but allowing a sense of calm and clarity to permeate our thoughts, actions and daily choices? What if resting in peace means not putting off joy and freedom until we die, but allowing ourselves to feel the full wonder of whatever it is we happen to be doing, or not doing, in every living moment?

72

*What if...*it's safe to open up?

There can be a lot of fear around opening oneself up. And with so much warring around the globe, it's hardly surprising. Why keeping our personal borders closed seems like the safer, wiser option. Perhaps we don't want to be invaded. Taken advantage of. Controlled. Hurt. We don't want to lose our identity. Our sovereignty. Letting our defences down can sometimes feel like the last thing we want to do. But what if being closed down is what harms us most in the end?

*What if...*it's safe to open up? What if it is only *through* opening up and sharing with each other, in daring to risk vulnerability, we discover our strength? Our true power. Not over others, but alongside others. What if, in opening up we see how connected we are? At a deep, deep level. How similar, even in our uniqueness. What if, rather than losing our identity, we discover our true identity? Not just Sovereign, but Divine. What if, ultimately, having the courage to open up is what stops all the warring? Both within and without.

73

What if...we've already arrived?

There is a lot of seeking going on in the world. Often involving a great deal of effort. We even say *trying to get somewhere in life. Soul searching.* It can be exhausting. Yet, in order to search for something, there is an assumption that we are separate from it. What if, ultimately, there's nowhere to go?

What if...we've already arrived? Here already. What if we've simply forgotten? What if all we truly seek is to remember? That despite our deepest regrets of the past and greatest fears about the future, right here, right now, in this moment, all is well. Over and over and over and over again.

74

*What if...*our pores are portals?

Detoxifying the body is a popular practice for those seeking better health. There are numerous ways of doing it, both simple and complex. Drinking water, colonic irrigation, sweat lodges, fasting, consuming unprocessed foods, to name but a few. Whichever way, it seems to be about unclogging the pores of the skin. But what if the power of detoxifying isn't just skin-deep (pun intended!) but cosmic?

*What if...*our pores are portals? Or, pore-tals! Quantum health practitioners speak of allowing healing light to enter our bodies. Life coaches speak of letting our light shine out. So what if the pores of our skin are gateways? Letting the light of the universe *in* and our divine light *out*. What if clearer pores allow this to happen more easily? Allow us to experience greater en-lighten-ment. What if one of the simplest ways to allow our pores to open is...to relax?

75

*What if...*countries have something to teach us?

We are used to being educated and informed. Whether it be by school teachers, the medical establishment, financial experts, scientists or spiritual gurus. We may even be open to our circumstances and relationships having something to teach us. But what if everything has the potential to deepen our understanding of who we are? For example...

*What if...*countries have something to teach us? Energetically, through the name of the country, the experience of its citizens, and how it relates to others. The United States of America, for example. Land of liberty and independence. Often referred to as the U.S. What if its biggest lesson is *Unity?* Not just U.S., but *Us.* We. Together. Not exclusively, but *inclusively.* For the benefit of All. What about the United Kingdom with its long history of royalty? A lesson in being *United in our Sovereignty*, perhaps. Reclaiming our power. Not over others, but alongside others. At this particular point in history, it seems the citizens of both nations, regardless of their leaders, have the unprecedented (or, perhaps, un-president-ed) opportunity to rise up and reclaim personal and collective sovereignty. To experience the true meaning of being *United.*

76

What if...each new generation keeps us current?

We often associate being older with being wiser; and though this is frequently the case, it isn't necessarily a given. As much as numerous years spent on this planet can create a wealth of wisdom, it can also lead to cynicism and a resistance to change. In some cases, an intolerance, disregard and disrespect toward younger generations.

What if...each new generation keeps us current? Keeps humanity moving forward. Up-to-date. In the present. Evolving. The value of youth being its *currency*. In every sense of the word. Since the lack of respect between the generations can go both ways, it is, perhaps, worth remembering one of two things; either we were the younger generation once, or will one day be the elders! Appreciating our inherent value, whatever our age.

77

*What if...*there are beings from other planets and galaxies?

Talk of a possible alien presence is usually guaranteed to evoke a look of concern on the faces of most people. Whether that be a concern for the mental health of the speaker, or inner fears regarding hostile invasion and human experimentation. Alien drama *is* a big hit at the box office! But what if there's nothing to fear?

*What if...*there are beings from other planets and galaxies? Beings who simply want to say hello. To connect with us. Like meeting a tribe on an undiscovered continent. Or long-lost family, perhaps. As interesting as it would be to hear about their experiences, what if they are equally curious to hear about ours? Imagine the reunion celebration!

78

What if...we die so life can go on?

Despite the inevitability, change can be difficult. If only life would stand still for five minutes so we could sit back and enjoy it! But no. Endings come. Losses happen. In the midst of the ensuing grief, life can feel so meaningless. The pain downright unnecessary. But what if there is a point to it all? Even our own death.

*What if...*we die so life can go on? Naturally creating space, as it were. Making room. Allowing movement. So we can all come around again. Choosing different roles. New experiences. Recycling at its best! What if all losses guide us toward a greater appreciation of life? Not just in hindsight, but in every passing moment. The smallest everyday endings — the end of a fine meal or a conversation with a friend, say — an opportunity to focus on gratitude for what is. Preparation, perhaps, for the ultimate change in life. Our own death. When we let go of our physical bodies, and literally trans*form* into something new. Not so much an ending as a beginning, then. A cause for celebration, even.

79

*What if...*we control our DNA?

DNA, found in every cell of our body, is said to contain biological information. Instructions that tell our bodies how to grow and function. Until now we have tended to think of our DNA as set in stone. Our blueprint for life. Often perceiving it as the cause of many health conditions and, in turn, any personal limitation we may experience as a result. However, new science is suggesting that far from being driven by our DNA, we are, in fact, the driver.

*What if...*we control our DNA? Not simply at the mercy of our genes, but rather co-creating partners. Mind and body together. Consciously affecting our own health and wellbeing at a molecular level. By bringing awareness to the endless possibilities and releasing old, self-limiting beliefs in the process. This union of mind and body being the ultimate relational experience of *chemistry*, perhaps.

80

*What if...*sometimes the only break we need is from ourselves?

Aaah! The thought of going away on holiday, taking a well-earned break, can bring a sense of imminent relief. As we look forward to escaping the pressures of everyday life. What a shame then, that for many, it only happens once or twice a year (if at all!) Our respite woefully short. With the financial cost and/or high expectations sometimes leaving us more stressed and disappointed than before we left, we might well wonder why bother holidaying at all?

*What if...*sometimes the only break we need is from ourselves? Our desire to take a break often being a response to the busyness of everyday life. A busyness often fuelled by an underlying fear that we're not quite good enough. Haven't quite achieved enough. That we're not quite there yet. But what if we recognised and acknowledged our worth, right now, just as we are? Totally valued ourselves and our experiences. Would we still feel as desperate to *get away from it all*? Would there be anything to get away from? What if sometimes all we really need to take a break from is the self-defeating chatter of our own minds? Something we can do any time, anywhere. Leaving us free to holiday just for the fun of it, and not because we *need* to.

81

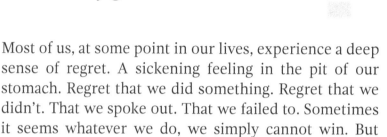

*What if...*we are free to start anew in any given moment?

Most of us, at some point in our lives, experience a deep sense of regret. A sickening feeling in the pit of our stomach. Regret that we did something. Regret that we didn't. That we spoke out. That we failed to. Sometimes it seems whatever we do, we simply cannot win. But what if the opposite is true?

*What if...*we are free to start anew in any given moment? Press the reset button. *Wipe the slate clean.* A momentary sense of regret can be helpful. It can guide us to make wiser choices. Help us see what works for us and what doesn't. Yet, to dwell too long can be self-defeating. It serves neither us nor those around us. Self-forgiveness, on the other hand, does! So what if it's possible to liberate ourselves at any time? Not just from regrets of the past, but fears about the future too. Continually releasing ourselves. Starting afresh. With a clear mind and an open heart.

82

What if...we possess the ability to teleport?

Scientists have reportedly teleported a particle over hundreds of kilometres to a satellite in space. Now before we all go clicking our fingers and sending ourselves to Hawaii, the quantum teleportation trials are said to be about the sending of information as opposed to solid objects. However, the very stuff of which we're made — atoms — are believed to be over 99.9% empty space and, at a quantum level, everything is said to be information. Including us. Hmm...

*What if...*we posses the ability to teleport? As science-fictional as it may sound, there have, across the ages, been various reports of people (including the Buddha himself) exhibiting the ability to teleport. Via one's state of being. What if the key, then, is not *out there*, but within us? Outer space exploration through deep inner space exploration, as it were. Our interior world a portal to the wider world (or worlds) around us. When it comes to instantaneous travel, however, it is perhaps worth pausing and remembering the joy of the journey... although it certainly beats queuing at the airport!

83

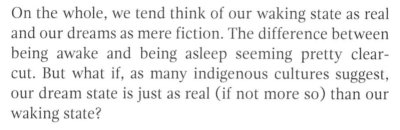

*What if...*life really is but a dream?

On the whole, we tend think of our waking state as real and our dreams as mere fiction. The difference between being awake and being asleep seeming pretty clear-cut. But what if, as many indigenous cultures suggest, our dream state is just as real (if not more so) than our waking state?

*What if...*life really is but a dream? As topsy-turvy as it may sound, it would certainly be an immense relief at times! Like, literally, waking up from a nightmare. Could this be what the process of awakening is really all about? If it were true, what difference might it make? Knowing life is not as 'real' as it seems. Once the initial shock and confusion subsided, would we be inspired to take things more easily? Lighten up a little. Or, as the nursery rhyme suggests, *row, row, row* our boats *gently down the stream?* A little more *merrily, merrily, merrily, merrily*, perhaps?

84

What if...the joy of relationship includes celebrating our uniqueness?

Can't live with 'em; can't live without 'em! Words often associated with the difficulties of being both *in* and *out* of relationship. Whether it be romantic partners, friends or family. In truth, an adage pointing to the challenges inherent in *all* relationships. Including our wider community and at a national level too. The pivotal question being: How do we come together without losing ourselves?

*What if...*the joy of relationship includes celebrating our uniqueness? Some might argue it's *all* about losing ourselves in the other. Merging. Becoming one. Especially when it comes to romance. And perhaps to some degree, it is. But what if it's equally about realising the value of our individuality? It can, however, take a great deal of courage to not deny or hide our unique selves in the company of others. To live our own personal values. Despite the pressure we sometimes feel to do otherwise. To be like everyone else. To conform. Perhaps stemming from the inherent desire to belong. To feel connected. What if, then, entering into any kind of relationship feeling *already connected* to something greater than our individual selves is precisely what gives us the confidence to express ourselves and relate in a way that is uniquely us?

85

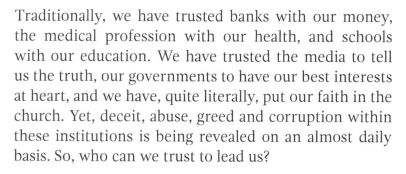

*What if...*it's time for us to lead ourselves?

Traditionally, we have trusted banks with our money, the medical profession with our health, and schools with our education. We have trusted the media to tell us the truth, our governments to have our best interests at heart, and we have, quite literally, put our faith in the church. Yet, deceit, abuse, greed and corruption within these institutions is being revealed on an almost daily basis. So, who can we trust to lead us?

*What if...*it's time for us to lead ourselves? To take responsibility both individually and collectively. To put the humanity back into Humanity. It was the Native American Hopi Elders who urged, *Do not look outside yourselves for the leader.* With the current and ongoing revelations, this advice is beginning to make sense. So what if it is possible for us everyday citizens of earth to come together? By-passing the old, corrupt systems to create a fairer, more honest and joy-filled world for ourselves. As the Hopi concluded...*this could be a good time!*

86

*What if...*there is no original thought?

We can sometimes feel quite precious and protective of our ideas. At times, it may even feel as if someone has stolen them from us. However, it's been said that everything we can possibly think of can exist; as nothing is new or what we call original thought. Hmm, tricky to imagine. Though on a positive note, it would certainly relieve the pressure of trying to come up with something new! And, by definition, would put plagiarists out of business! All joking aside, if it's true, what's the significance?

*What if...*there is no original thought? We are certainly not islands. We have been absorbing information since the day we were conceived. Whether it be via family, friends, school, society, books, television, and the internet (to name but a few), everything we have ever learned has come through someone or something else. Even the deepest inspiration from within often appears to stem from something bigger than ourselves. A greater source. What if, then, we are simply recirculating and recycling what already is? Coming up with our own combinations and unique ways of expressing the same thing. What if what already is...*is Love*? Thankfully not an original thought!

87

*What if...*we are all connected?

We certainly appear to be separate. Individual beings. Set apart. Science is, however, discovering that our personal energy field extends far beyond our physical body. We are, therefore, intermingling at an energetic level whether we realise it or not. Who knows how far we interconnect in truth? What if it's all the way?

*What if...*we are all connected? Swirls of energy all dancing together. Co-creating worlds. We may seem to be having our own individual experience (and at one level, we are), but, in truth, we are constantly affecting and being affected by each other. By the Whole. Consciously or unconsciously. Whether we like it or not. The shared witnessing of global events, for example, whether tragic or spectacular, is (in many instances) bringing us together in larger numbers than ever before. Reminding us we are at once, individual and unified. Not apart from but a part of.

88

*What if...*more is our natural state?

On the one hand, we are led to believe the more we have, do, and are, the better. More qualifications, more money, more holidays, more friends, more social approval, and so on. On the other hand, from a moral point of view, many of us feel bad about wanting more. It seems selfish. Inconsiderate. Greedy.

*What if...*more is our natural state? Not necessarily accumulating more 'stuff', more personal glory, but greater awareness of what we already are. What if, as scientists are discovering, that despite outer appearances, everything in the universe is made of essentially the same thing? That we originate from a single source. What if, then, our true desire for more is a natural urge to remember our inherent Wholeness? That we are *already more* than we can possibly conceive from our individual perspective.

89

What if... 'heaven' is here?

Oh, what a funny one! A shocker, right? *Only the truly insane would consider this to be heaven!* Whatever our definition of heaven may be, it is, perhaps, difficult to imagine this being it. Sure, there is a lot of beauty on the planet, but there's also so much violence and war. Still, what if what we ultimately seek really is *right under our nose*?

What if... 'heaven' is here? Whether we realise it or not. What if realising it depends on where we place our focus? That is, *where we choose to place our focus determines our reality*. Both individually and together. So, are we focusing on the Beauty, the Connectedness, the Love? Or are we focusing, instead, on the ugliness, the isolation and the fear? What if focusing on the latter, even with the best of intentions, is the very thing that perpetuates it? What if we are here, not to seek someone else's definition of heaven, but to create our own personal version? Based on what brings us joy. Connects us. Allows us to feel and share love in our own unique way. Imagine, infinite versions of heaven-on-earth being created simultaneously. Heavenly!

90

What if...we are God?

Imagine...we happen to glance down at our hands one day, only to notice one hand, a little like a glove puppet, nervously introducing itself to the other. The other hand, likewise, responding with a timid *Hello*. As if perfect strangers. Meeting for the first time. From our vantage point *up above*, it would seem utterly ridiculous. Complete madness. But what if this is us? Thinking we are separate. Unaware we are one body. Entirely connected. One.

*What if...*we are God? Creation Itself. All of us together. Along with everything else. It is, perhaps, the most thought-provoking and highly divisive *What if...?* question of all. The mere notion considered blasphemous, downright crazy, and scary as hell to some. Making perfect sense, feeling like divine truth, and bringing immense relief to others. But what if we are God experiencing Oneself in a multitude of ways? Trying out life; this way and that. Choosing to separate Oneself into individual aspects (us) just for the thrill of coming back together. Reuniting. Again and again. One big cosmic inhale and exhale. *And...breathe!*

Creating Your Own
What if...? Questions

Thank you for joining me on this weird and wonderful journey of examining, questioning and exploring our currently held beliefs. I hope it has been as helpful to you as it has been to me. In the process of compiling this book, I realised I was creating a personal resource. A self-support system. My own 'book of answers', as it were. Not only did creating the questions help in the present moment, they became a resource I could look back on any time. Something solid, physical and reliable that I could turn to whenever I was feeling troubled. I would simply choose a number at random and read the question. It's uncanny how, no matter the concern, the question that came up was just right. It helped me lighten up in an instant. The beauty and the potency of creating one's own collection of *What if...?* questions is that they are, by nature, tailor-made to one's own habitual and recurring patterns and blocks. For this reason, they are resourceful over and over again. Helping us to address and release our own unique set of limitations.

In retrospect, it's remarkable how long it took me to fully appreciate this. To realise creating the book was helping me in my everyday life – when I remembered to *read* it as well as write it! In this way, the book was actually helping me to write the book. Talk about self-sustaining! This is what I wish for you too. That you discover you have the wisdom to answer all your own questions. Although this book embraces the power of 90 days, it doesn't matter how many questions you create, as even 7 core questions can be deeply transformative. And remember, you can always turn your questions into 'oracle cards' for instant guidance by bringing awareness to what is troubling you in the present moment, randomly choosing a number, or closing your eyes and flicking through the pages until you feel the urge to stop, and reading that question. So, whether you decide to create your own *What if...?* questions solely for present moment concerns — as and when they arise — or whether you would like to create your own book of *What if...?* questions as an ongoing resource, here are some simple guidelines that have helped me, followed by a seven-step template to creating your own *What if...?* questions.

Things to consider

Keeping it present moment

In creating this book, I was tempted to write the pages in advance and, yet, I noticed the easiest and most powerful way was to observe actual present moment concerns as they arose on a daily basis. So start with noticing what is troubling you in *this* moment.

Keeping it simple

There may be a number of things troubling you right now, but keep it simple by focusing on just one issue at a time. The most pressing, perhaps.

Taking personal responsibility

Many problems appear to stem from other people and, of course, they are part of the equation but rather than focusing on how others are behaving or feeling, always bring the focus back to oneself. How am *I* behaving or feeling? This is not about blaming oneself but about taking personal responsibility. Rather than trying to change others, or the world around us, acknowledging our the part in the problem is what gives us the power to change it.

Writing it down

A sense of routine and structure is helpful, particularly in the initial stages. For example, writing down questions in a journal on a regular basis can provide a sense of ground, connection and purpose. Eventually you may find writing it down is no longer necessary. That you are able to quickly and effortlessly flip unhelpful thoughts into their most powerful opposites, as they arise. Simply by taking a few moments and a few deep breaths to recognise and mentally re-write your beliefs. But, for now (and certainly for the purpose of creating one's own collection of *What if...?* questions as a resource), write it down.

Turning it into its *What if...?* opposite

As strange as it may sound, this stage can sometimes feel a little challenging. Imagining and opening up to unlimited possibilities can, initially, feel a little ridiculous, pointless, overwhelming, or just downright unfamiliar. However, this is a great opportunity to practise letting go and opening up in the safety of your own mind/personal space.

Noticing what happens

Once you've created your *What if...?* alternative, imagine, however briefly, that it is true. Notice how it feels physically, emotionally, mentally, or even spiritually. In time, observe yourself in relationship to others and the world around you as you explore how this change of perception affects your reality. Are your worst fears borne out? Or were they baseless? Some of mine were borne out! For example, I feared if I were truthful, no matter how compassionately, people might leave. Some did. Yet, the relationships with those who stayed continue to go from strength to strength, deepening in ways I couldn't have imagined. So even those fears that came to pass were strangely validating. Either way, it is vital information that helps us begin to choose our experience and create our preferred reality.

Seven Steps to Creating Your Own
What if...? Questions

On the following pages you will find prompts and space to help you create your own *What if...?* questions, as well as extra space at the back of the book.

1. What is troubling you most right now? This could be an inner fear about oneself, an issue in relationship to others, or a concern about the world in general. You can write it down in the space below.

2. Create one simple sentence that gets to the heart of the problem. Beginning with "*I...*"

Example 1: *I am just not clever enough.*

Example 2: *I am angry that I didn't get the promotion.*

Example 3: *I am devastated that the country is going to war again.*

3. Flip this sentence into its ideal opposite. Remember there is no right or wrong here. There are infinite possibilities, but what is your *preferred* reality?

Example 1: *I am just not clever enough* might be transformed into *What if...I know all I need to know?*

Example 2: *I am angry that I didn't get the promotion* might become *What if...I didn't get the promotion because something even better wants to come into my life?*

Example 3: *I am devastated that the country is going to war again* might be flipped into *What if...all the pain and suffering of war is ultimately propelling humanity into making wiser and more peaceful choices for all?*

You have just created your working title.

4. Now notice all the reasons why this simply cannot be true. Write down your fears, resistances, blocks and *Yeah but's*.

Example 1: *Everybody else knows more than me. I'm too slow to learn. I've missed my chance. It's too late now.*

Example 2: *I never get promoted! Those bosses are useless. I'm always being overlooked and taken for granted. It was bound to be a man that got the job. She only got chosen for her looks. Maybe I'm just not good enough.*

Example 3: *We're doomed! This can't possibly lead to peace! I'm powerless!*

You have just created your first paragraph.

5. Write a sentence or two considering, exploring, or playing with alternative possibilities. Be as wild, imaginative, loving or gentle as you like.

Example 1: *Perhaps judging myself stops me from even listening. Maybe I don't need to know what other people know. Perhaps I can just take an interest in the things that bring me joy. Maybe I always know enough to take me to the next step.*

Example 2: *Was that promotion really the best thing for me, especially since I really don't enjoy working for those bosses? Am I even in the right kind of job? Perhaps this happened to urge me to find more rewarding work?*

Example 3: *What can I do to help create world peace? Am I helping by coming from a place of fear and powerlessness, or am I creating more of it? Perhaps developing inner peace sends out a more peaceful, calming vibe to those around me? What if, in this way, I am contributing to a more peaceful household, community, and ultimately, world?*

There is space over the page to write.

You have just created your second, and final, paragraph.

6. **Notice how these possibilities affect you physically, emotionally, mentally or even spiritually.** For example, has your breathing altered? Have your shoulders, your chest, neck, jaw or any other part of your body relaxed in any way? Are you feeling any lighter emotionally, or clearer of mind? Is there a deeper sense of peace or connection, perhaps? You don't have to do anything about it. It is simply an exercise in awareness. Helping us make more aligned choices.

7. Check: Are you happy with your original title?

Occasionally, we may feel we've identified a problem, only to discover it's really about something else completely. For example, a concern that initially appears to be about a relationship may, ultimately, be about self-worth. On these occasions, feel free to alter your working title if, on reflection, it feels more fitting.

Congratulations! Your *What if...?* question is complete.

If you would like to create more of your own *What if...?* questions, you will find space at the end of this book.

Bibliography

Zen And The Pen: How to write a book in 90 days (Robert Christopher, Cottage Press 2013)

Although only one book was directly referenced in the writing of this book there is an infinite number of books and articles that have served as a constant source of inspiration to me. Below are just a few of my favourites — ones that relate, in particular, to beliefs and the nature of reality.

Further Reading:

The Biology Of Belief: Unleashing the Power of Consciousness, Matter & Miracles — Bruce Lipton, (Hay House 2015)

The Spontaneous Healing Of Belief: Shattering the Paradigm of False Limits — Gregg Braden, (Hay House (Reprint edition) 2009)

Reality Is Not What It Seems: The Journey to Quantum Gravity — Carlo Rovelli, (Penguin Books, 2016)

Additional links:

Death Of A Genius: Life magazine, May 2, 1955 p.64

https://books.google.co.uk/books?id=dlYEAAAAMBAJ& printsec=frontcover&source=gbs_ge_summary_r&cad=0

A Belief is Just a Thought You Keep Thinking — Abraham-Hicks

https://www.youtube.com/watch?v=q99MxSz3Qgw

Ground-to-satellite quantum teleportation

https://arxiv.org/pdf/1707.00934v1.pdf

Acknowledgements

Thank you to my wonderful family for lovingly supporting me with blind faith, as well as time and space to create; Caroline for her unwavering support from the beginning, and for introducing me to the lovely Sarah; who in turn put me in touch with the amazing editor, Emma – whose support and presence is phenomenal. Big thanks to publisher, Sarah, at Goldcrest Books, for getting this book across the finish line and making it a reality. Special thanks to Lauren and all the wonderful staff at the Sherwood Pines Cafe, Nottinghamshire, for continually providing a delightful atmosphere in which to create.

About the Author

Originally trained in a depth, Buddhist-based psychotherapy, Marie consciously stepped off her chosen career path in order to practise all she had learned on a daily basis; a journey that continues to be a constant source of inspiration that permeates her writing. Marie enjoys exploring the nature of reality and practically applying all she discovers. An advocate of discovering one's true nature, through nature, Marie also leads a weekly walking meditation group through the woodland trails of Sherwood Forest — currently celebrating its fifth year.

If you would like to share your *What if...?* experience, please feel free to do so at www.mariescott.net

What if...? Notes

What if...? Notes

What if...? Notes

What if...? Notes

What if...? Notes

What if...? Notes

What if...? Notes

What if...? Notes

What if...? Notes

What if...? Notes

What if...? Notes

What if...? Notes